German Railroad Guns in action

by Joachim Engelmann

Illustrated by Don Greer

Edited by Bruce Culver

squadron/signal publications

"Anzio Annie", as the 28cm K5(E) railway gun as known to the Allies, fires into the Allied beachead at Anzio. The Germans knew this gun as 'Schanke Bertha' and nicknamed it 'Leopold.'

1115 CROWLEY DRIVE, CARROLLTON, TEXAS 75006

ISBN 0-89747-048-6

Originally published in Germany as "Deutsche Eisenbahngeschütze" by Podzun-Verlag, 636 Freidberg-3/Dorheim, Markt 9, West Germany.

Photo Credits

Bundesarchiv Koblenz
Archiv Engelmann
Archiv Podzun-Verlag
Beinhauer
Rail Gun (Skizzen)
John Batchelor Ltd,
Broadstone, Dorset

RAILROAD GUNS

Railroad guns are a very interesting part of the history of artillery development since the American Civil War. Modern technology has made these giant weapons obsolete, but for a number of years, in different conflicts, railway artillery played an important role in providing military forces with mobile heavy guns capable of breaching heavy fortifications or shelling strategic targets at long range. Movable coastal defense batteries were also used to supplement fixed defensive guns during invasions.

The railroad was the first development in transportation with the rise of the Machine Age, and allowed the movement of mounted heavy guns long before self-propelled carriages, engines, or roads existed. Railroad artillery was dependent on the availability of an extensive railway network for the greatest mobility--a disadvantage never entirely overcome--but in the later years of railroad gun development, this was offset to a great extent by the greater destructive effect of ever larger projectiles and by significant increases in maximum range, which often allowed large areas to be controlled by only a few guns. Characterized by relatively long barrels compared to other forms of artillery--many of these taken over from naval weapons production--and mounted on specially-modified or purpose-built railroad cars or carriages, the railroad guns proved to be excellent heavy artillery pieces, and were moved relatively easily despite their size.

Only 28 years after the beginning of a useful railway system in 1825, the first extensive plan for arming railroad trains appeared in England. However, the plan envisaged mounted weapons for defense of troop and supply trains, rather than the later offensive use of long range artillery. 12 years later, during the final months of the American Civil War, March/April 1865, a primitive 32 cm drilled cast steel mortar was mounted on a reinforced flat car and used with considerable success in the capture of Richmond, the Confederate Capital.

Later, up to World War II, many nations would use developments of the original English proposal for armed trains for defense–by both sides during the Russian Civil War; by the French, to support the Maginot Line; by the English to protect the southern coast during the threat of German invasion across the Channel; and by the Germans, to combat partisans in Russia and other occupied countries. The lack of mobility was most keenly felt in these antipartisan duties.

Around 1900, France and England in particular had good railroad networks that could be developed for artillery use, and the U.S.A. also had a good railroad system, ideally suited for placing coastal defense guns. Germany had a dense railroad network well-suited for the use of railway artillery, but Germany had also developed efficient heavy field pieces, and as a result, little demand existed for railroad guns and except for a few designs by Krupp, virtually no development was undertaken before 1914.

With the start of the Great War and the mobilization of millions of men, there soon were demands for railway artillery to supplement the current heavy field artillery. Many various designs were tried. Development of naval rifles (heavy naval guns) for battleships and cruisers of the German Navy (as also done by England and France) resulted in many improvements in barrels, projectiles, and propellants. In Germany most of the early guns came from the reserve stocks for the Navy, or from older naval vessels. Krupp's Essen works, the producer of heavy gun barrels for the Navy, became responsible for developing and producing most of the railroad artillery; the various types were all given names, which identified the class of weapon.

The 17 cm cannon "Samuel" was an improvised structure using an existing barrel and modified carriage, but the 21 cm "Peter Adalbert" gun proved excellent as a standard design. The 28 cm "Bruno" design introduced a built-in gun carriage turntable on top of the railroad carriage so that the gun could be traversed a full 360°. "Bruno" class guns could be emplaced and prepared for firing in only one day. The heaviest standard gun was the 38 cm "Max", which was used at Verdun and Dunkirk. The largest weapon was the 21 cm "Paris" gun, refined from a design by Dr. V. Eberhard, and constructed with the assistance of Admiral Rogge, of the Naval weapons department. A total of 7 "Paris" guns were supposed to have been built.

The period following World War I was one of development and was devoted to solving the problems of traversing large guns, and of absorbing the recoil forces in the carriage. Several different designs were tried. The sliding recoil absorbing system involved lowering the gun carriage onto the tracks instead of having a special recoil system on the carriage. When the gun was fired, the whole carriage slid backwards along the rails. A second system simply allowed the carriage to roll freely to the rear when the gun was fired; the brakes stopped it after a short run. A third system used outrigger stabilizers to relieve the railroad carriages of the shock from absorbing the recoil forces, while the gun–mounted on a rotating platform independent of the railroad carriage–could be traversed in any direction during firing. The stabilizers enabled even broadside firing without danger.

Larger guns, too big for on-carriage turntables, could be traversed across a target front by using a section of curved track. The carriage was pushed along the curve until the barrel of the gun was pointed toward the target. Aiming stakes driven into the roadbed allowed the weapon to be placed on target following firing, as the carriage usually moved back during recoil. The German Wehrmacht in World War II did not use the above system very often after the development of the VÖGELE turntable, which was dismantled and transported with the gun to the firing point. Erected in place, the VÖGELE turntable could accommodate loads of 80 to 180 tonnen, and by allowing the railway artillery to fire in any direction–a full 360° field of fire–it enabled one or two guns to support troops and control strongpoints over a fairly large area.

After 1933, the construction department for railway artillery at Krupp, which had been only 20 people, was increased to over 2,000. Erich Müller (later Professor Müller) was assigned as manager of the artillery branch, having been company director of the Berlin-Tempelhof works of the German national railroad. Müller brought with him valuable experience in various test departments of the railroad, especially in methods for shrinking steel in construction of equipment. In many instances, Krupp was able to refer back to the experiences in World War I, and by using available Naval rifle barrels, again on improvised carriages, was able to expand production to meet the 1936 program. Technical advances resulted in many improvements: several types of recoil systems and recuperators; hydraulic elevation of the upper carriage; electrically powered traverse and ammunition loading mechanisms; and the introduction of the VÖGELE turntable design. These new railroad guns were used for concentrated support fire during advances, and also for coastal defense duties.

Until 1944, the guns carried the markings: "DESSART" (very heavy artillery); "Berlin W15" (location of the Army weapons department); "DEUTSCHE REICHSBAHN BERLIN" with a 6-digit number. All railroad rolling stock, including the carriages for the guns, was the responsibility of the German national railroad system, which supplied not only the locomotives and train crews, but also engineers and mechanics to service the gun carriages, brakes, etc. The weapons and laying equipment were the responsibility of the Artillery branch of the Army, and the emplacement of the gun, erection of turntables, defensive buttresses, camouflage measures, etc. was the responsibility of the railroad pioneers.

Only after 1938 did the newer guns begin to improve the capabilities of the artillery units, with designs like the 28 cm "New Bruno", 28 cm K5 (E) and the 21 cm K12 (E) and other types. At the same time the Oberkommando Heer (OKH) was demanding yet further increases in size, projectile weight, and maximum range. After 1940, captured railroad guns, mostly French weapons, were incorporated into German artillery units to increase the number of guns available.

Railway Artillery Regiments

In May 1940, there were 9 railroad artillery regiments, numbered: 676, 679, 680, 681, 702, 720, 766, 780, and 781. The batteries were divided as follows:

Number of Batteries	Type of Gun	Battery Numbers	Number of guns In All Batteries	Available as of 1 June 1941
1	15 cm	655	2 guns/batt. = 2	1 battery
2	17 cm	717, 718	3 guns/batt. = 6	2 batteries
1	21 cm	701	1 gun / batt. = 1	1 battery
4	24 cm	664, 674 721, 722	2 guns/batt. = 4 1 + 2 = 3	3 batteries
8	28 cm	688-690, 694-696, 710, 712	2+1 reserve = 17	13 batteries (some had only 1 gun)
16			33 guns	20 batteries

Note especially the increase in the number of 28 cm batteries from 1940 to 1941. On 22 June 1941--the start of "Barbarossa"--the batteries were deployed as follows: Eastern Front: southern sector-2; central sector-5; northern sector-2; Balkans-1; Western Front-9; Rügenwalde-1. At the same time, there were 13 armored trains, numbered: 1-7, 15, 21-25. In 1942, five railroad guns were built (USA: 50 guns built); in 1943, four guns (USA: 130); 1944 USA railroad gun production was 450. As a compensation for their fewer guns, the German railway artillery units had the heaviest and best weapons in the world.

There was much less need for railroad artillery during World War II. The war fronts were more fluid, there were fewer stationary strong points that required very heavy artillery, and advances in ballistics and heavy motor transport had resulted in the development of mobile (towed) heavy field artillery.

In addition, the large size and limited mobility of these large railroad weapons made them vulnerable to air attacks, which necessitated the deployment of auxiliary light flak units, smoke generators, and defense troops to protect the guns and support trains. Severe damage to rear area railroad trackage could trap the guns, and several of these had to be destroyed to prevent capture when they couldn't be withdrawn. During sustained actions, even concrete embrasures and bunkers were built for the gun crews and support personnel and supplies. Although partisan sabotage added to the problems of keeping the tracks open on the Eastern Front, the railroad guns were quite successful in this theatre of operations. Later, however, increased air attacks and the use of heavier, more destructive bombs did impair their effectiveness by destroying tracks, bridges, locomotives, and occasionally even the guns or carriages themselves.

The main disadvantages of the railroad guns were: lack of mobility across country, being confined to railroad tracks; susceptibility to detection or sabotage; danger of capture resulting from extensive destruction of the railroad network; the damage to the tracks from the firing and the heavy weight of the guns; the limited target area, especially of the early guns; and the need for more elaborate preparations for firing than was true of most field artillery.

The advantages of the guns, especially the later, larger models, were: easy mobility compared to the great size and weight of the pieces; the large caliber and great range of these guns; the great distance from most target areas, which meant that often the gun was never seen by the enemy; lighter weight compared to naval weapons of the same caliber and range; and the stable firing characteristics resulting from the high weight of the carriage and barrel, and the fact that most of these guns fired at high angles, directing the recoil forces downward.

Between 1914 and 1945, railway artillery formed a mobile reserve of very heavy artillery for most European armies, and also among the Allies. Many strongly fortified, heavily defended targets were captured with the use of these heavy weapons. Though made increasingly vulnerable to air attack and sabotage to the rail network at their best, the German railroad guns served effectively through World War II. Perhaps the most famous German guns—the "Paris" gun of WW I, and "Anzio Annie" of WW II—were not effectively countered while they were used. The "Paris" gun's design exceeded the German's abilities in ballistics, and though the gun had a very great range, accuracy was insufficient for true military purposes. "Anzio Annie", a 28 cm K5 (E) named "Leopold", shelled the Anzio beachhead unmercifully for weeks, inflicting heavy losses in men and material and its hiding place in a railroad tunnel proved an effective and safe cover. Undiscovered during the bombardment of the beach, "Leopold" was blown up by the Germans to prevent its capture intact, along with a second K5(E), "Robert". Rebuilt in the USA with parts from "Robert," "Leopold" now sits on a siding at Aberdeen Proving Ground, an impressive reminder of these giant weapons, once used with such devestating effect in the two great wars of this century.

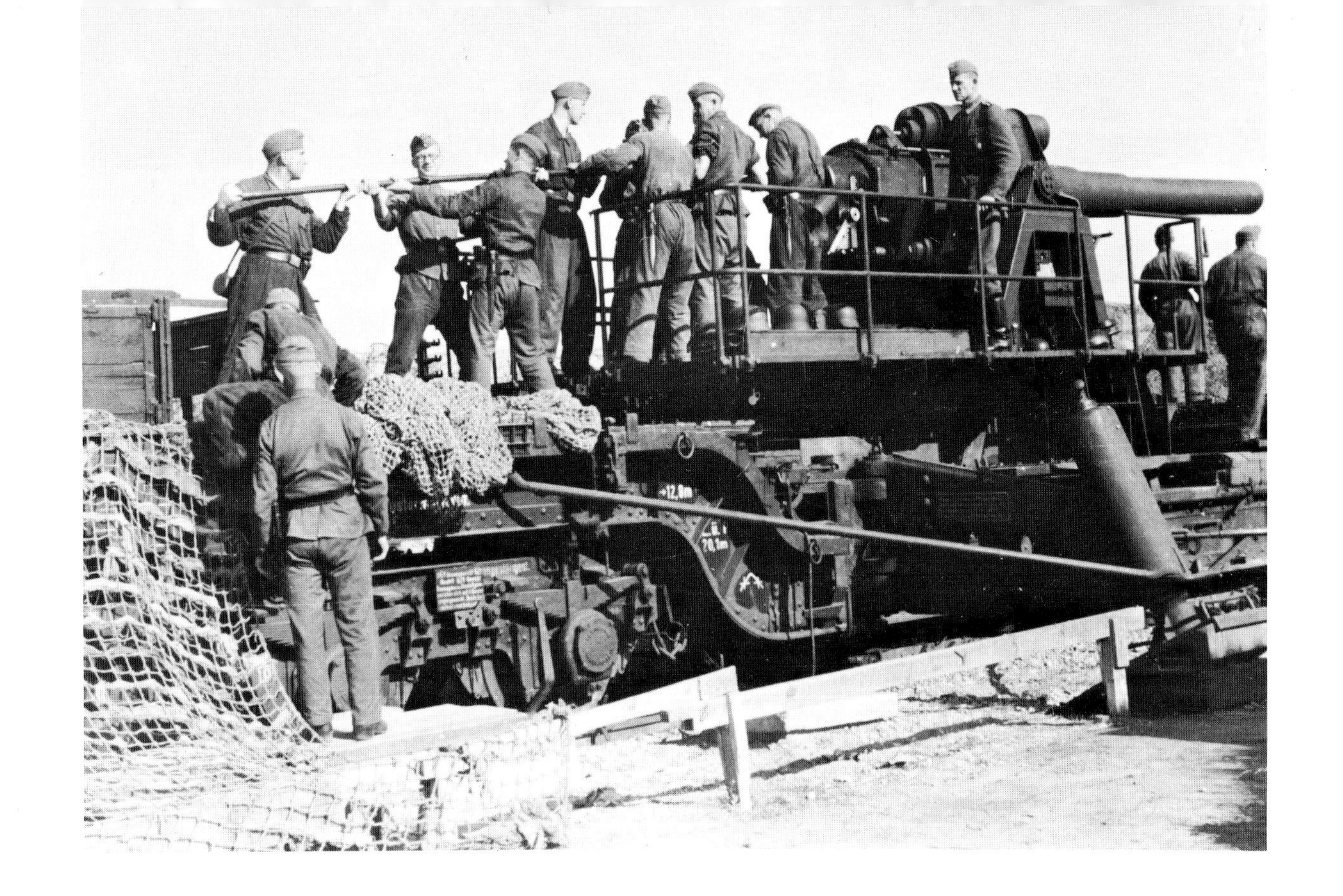

A 15 cm gun seen as the crew prepares to ram home a projectile. All large guns like this used separate ammunition—the shell was loaded first, then the propellant charge and casing, the latter serving to seal the breech. Note the swung-out stabilizer and bracing rod, which allowed full traverse and firing. Overhead clearance requirements and the need for the lowest possible center of gravity necessitated the use of a depressed-center carriage. Weight distribution required two 6-wheel trucks to prevent damage to the track.

Railroad battery 655 with two 15 cm guns in position ready to fire. These guns were constructed using 15 cm naval rifle barrels and fired a 43 kg shell at a muzzle velocity of 875 m/sec with a maximum range of 11.3 km to 22.5 km. The range was altered by using one of 3 different propellant charges. 18 of these weapons were built until 1938, when production was halted.

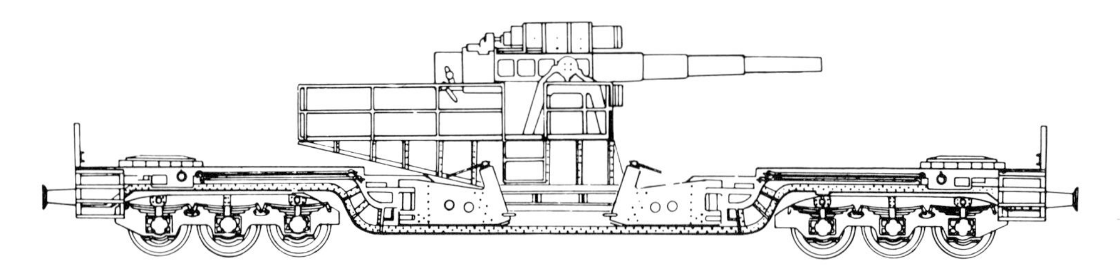

A side view drawing of the 15 cm railway gun. With a total weight of 74 tonnen, a barrel length of 5.69 meters, and a total length over the end buffers of 20.10 meters, this weapon was dropped from the production program, as the effort and materials needed for construction was more than the limited effectiveness of this weapon was worth. In the meantime, comparable 15 cm and 17 cm field artillery had been developed, eliminating the need for these smaller railroad guns.

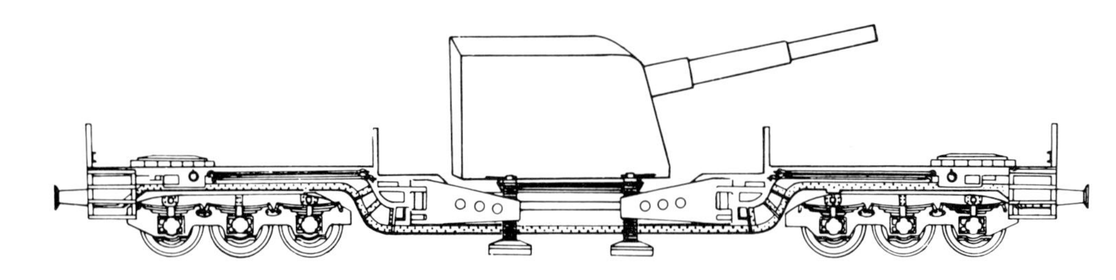

15 cm railroad battery "Gneisenau," seen here as part of the crew cleans out the barrel. Note the open breechblock and firing lanyard, and the loading ramrod lying on the side platform. On these railway guns, ship's armored turrets [open casement type] have been installed over the standard 15 cm mounts.

15 cm guns of the "Gneisenau" battery. This unit was part of the German Navy—all others belonged to the Army. The guns formed part of the defense in the West, and are seen here in 1944, in France.

Four 15 cm SK L/40 guns of the "Gneisenau" naval battery, showing the extended side stabilizers. Maximum range was achieved with 45° elevation of the barrels, and the battery of 4 guns could deliver 80 rounds on a target in one hour.

This side view drawing of the 17 cm railway gun shows the great similarity to the 15 cm design, especially in the gun carriage and railroad trucks. The major new component was the barrel, 1.21 m longer than that of the 15 cm. Muzzle velocity was 875 m/sec and muzzle energy 2517 m/tonnen. Compared to the 15 cm railroad gun, the 17 cm design weighed 6 tonnen more, and threw a shell only 7.8 kg more than the 15 cm projectile. Maximum range was 26.8 km, 4.3 km more than the 15 cm gun.

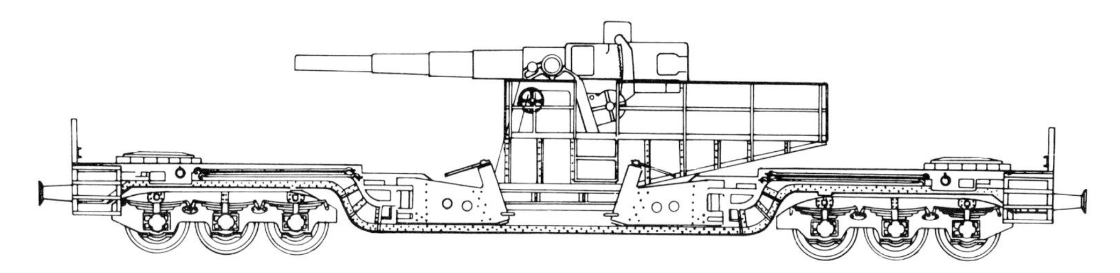

17 cm

A 17 cm railroad gun seen in a marshaling yard in France, 1942. The stabilizer arms have been swung out to the sides. Batteries 717 and 718 were formed having three 17 cm guns each. The 17 cm railroad gun was discontinued after limited production because it offered only a marginal improvement in performance over the 15 cm weapons. Even with the advantage of 360° traverse, the small increase in range and projectile weight was insufficient to justify the effort needed to manufacture these guns.

20,3 cm

[Below] The more modern 20.3 cm railroad gun with an L/60 barrel, was built from 1936, and until 1941 was designated SK C/34. The weight was 86.1 tonnen, the barrel length was 12.15 m., and overall carriage length was only 19.44 m. The 122 kg projectile was fired at a muzzle velocity of 925 m/sec., giving a maximum range of 36.4 km--exceeding the 30 km range desired by the Army. Eight of these guns were constructed, using extra barrels manufactured for the "Blücher" class heavy cruisers ["Blücher," "Admiral Hipper," "Prinz Eugen"], and were considered a very successful improvisation. The barrels were eventually supposed to be replaced with 21 cm K38 barrels, as 20.3 was a non-standard bore size in the Army. The recoil system was beneath the barrel near the breech.

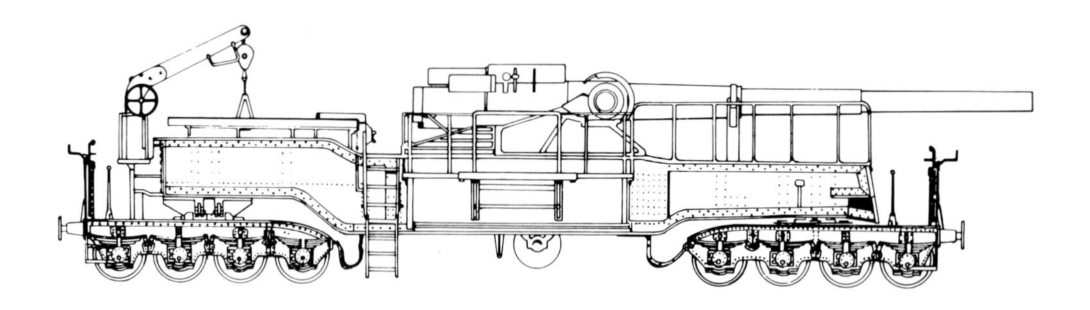

The 20.3 cm railroad gun with its longer L/60 barrel, weighing 20.7 tonnen. Note the replacement of the rotating gun turntable with a fixed carriage that allowed elevation only. Because of the increased weight, an extra axle was added to each railroad truck, and an ammunition crane was fitted due to the heavier ammunition. The maximum elevation was 47° and the gun could be used on a VÖGELE turntable, giving 360° traverse. Six of these 20.3 cm weapons were captured by the Allies in 1944 during the liberation of France.

An unique photo showing the transport of a 20.3 cm Kanone [E]. Rather than lay track up to the intended emplacement site, it was possible, with the smaller guns, to move them by road. Two specially constructed 24-wheel trailers were necessary for this operation. Note that while the work was being observed by Wehrmacht troops, the actual movement was done by civilian Reichsbahn workers.

Front view of the 21 cm K12 [E] being moved into its firing position. The long barrel overhung the end of the carriage, which has been raised on hydraulic jacks to provide adequate clearance for recoil movement. Note also the heavy cast connecting link that attached the gun carriage to the buffer system of the VÖGELE turntable. The buffer system absorbed most of the recoil force and limited the length of the recoil roll during firing. The muzzle velocity from the L/196 barrel was 1625 m/sec., and the bracing to keep the barrel from bending under its own weight can be seen alongside the barrel tube.

The hydraulic jacks, shown here under the ends of the gun carriage, were needed to raise the carriage up to one meter. This was necessitated by the long recoil travel of the barrel at high angles of fire, as there was a real danger of the breechblock recoiling too far and smashing into the ground or the tracks. Maximum elevation of the 33.3 m long barrel was 55°, and with the raised jacks, the full range of elevation could be used. With the velocity measuring troop [mot] 607, the single 21 cm K12[E] formed the E-Batterie 701.

Here the very heavy barrel of the K12[E] is still in travel order, lying supported in the cradle on the gun carriage. Though three guns were planned, only two were constructed—in view of the improved capabilities of the Luftwaffe bomber formations, the special missions for the K12[E], bombarding England across the Channel, became irrelevant. By the end of 1940, the two guns had been implaced on the French coast and did shell Dover, Folkestone, and—until 1941—parts of Kent.

21 cm

The massive, heavy breech, here with the breechblock closed, served as a counterweight to the extremely long barrel. The great weight of the breech assembly allowed the trunnions to be mounted near the rear of the barrel, resulting in higher permissible angles of fire and a lower center of gravity. Unfortunately, the waste in materials and production effort was a serious disadvantage of this weapon. In spite of this, the 21 cm K12[E] was a first class example of the state of the art in ballistics and engineering at the time of design and construction.

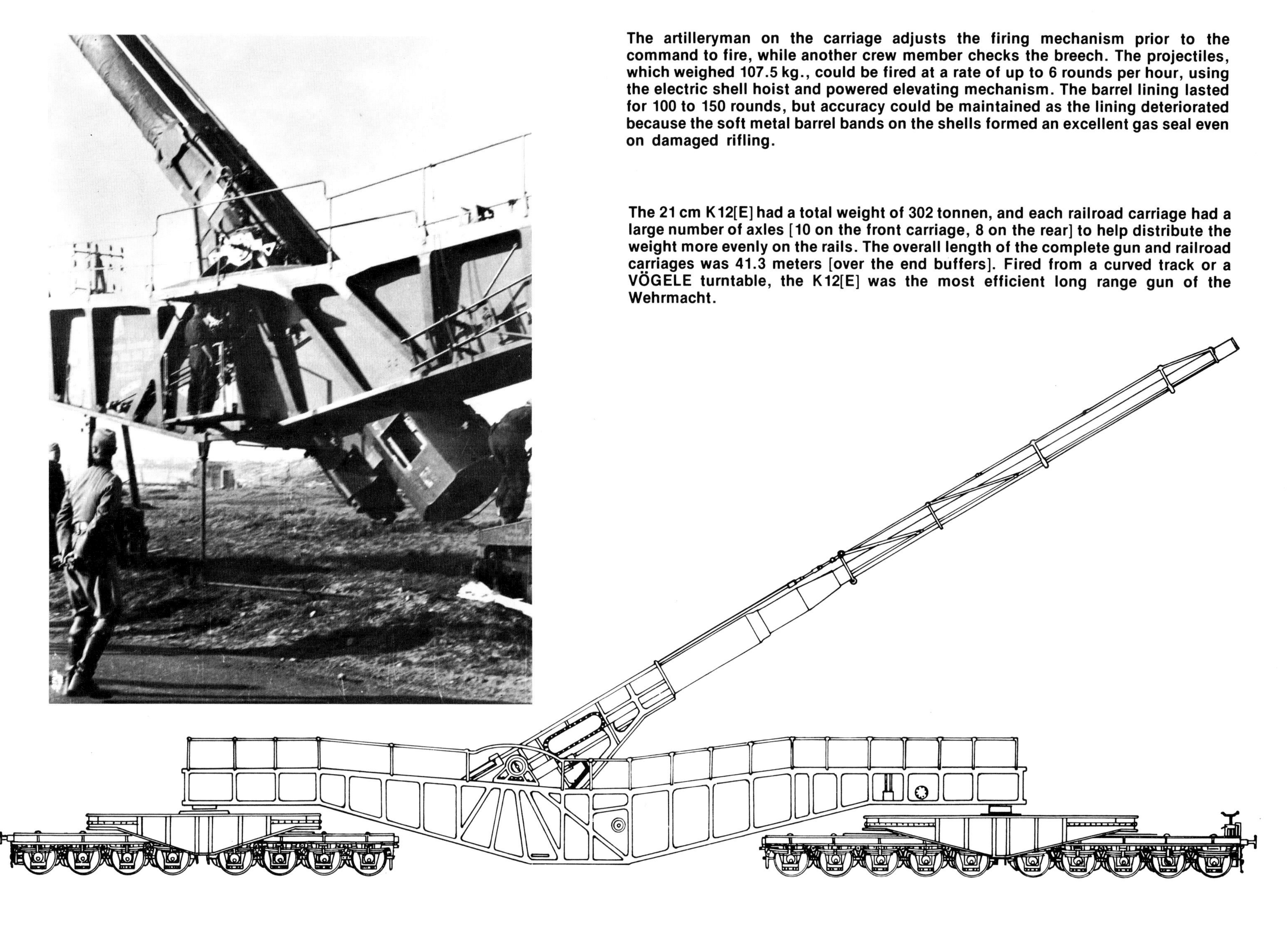

The artilleryman on the carriage adjusts the firing mechanism prior to the command to fire, while another crew member checks the breech. The projectiles, which weighed 107.5 kg., could be fired at a rate of up to 6 rounds per hour, using the electric shell hoist and powered elevating mechanism. The barrel lining lasted for 100 to 150 rounds, but accuracy could be maintained as the lining deteriorated because the soft metal barrel bands on the shells formed an excellent gas seal even on damaged rifling.

The 21 cm K12[E] had a total weight of 302 tonnen, and each railroad carriage had a large number of axles [10 on the front carriage, 8 on the rear] to help distribute the weight more evenly on the rails. The overall length of the complete gun and railroad carriages was 41.3 meters [over the end buffers]. Fired from a curved track or a VÖGELE turntable, the K12[E] was the most efficient long range gun of the Wehrmacht.

The 21 cm K12[E] long range gun normally had a firing range of 115 km., and with subcaliber ammunition up to 140 km. This rear view, taken in the West in 1944, shows the extremely long barrel and the necessary bracing system to keep it from bending under its own weight—this was a fault shared with the "Paris" gun of WW I, which was designed by Prof. Rausenberger and inspired the design of the K12[E]. With a compressed air double action recoil system, the total recoil travel was only 98 cm. The original idea for these very long range guns came from Dr. von Eberhardt in 1916. He was able to improve the range of long guns by increasing the muzzle velocity which sent the projectile into the stratosphere, where the thin air allowed the shells to travel much farther, resulting in ranges of more than 100 km.

Specifications

	15cmK	17cmK	20cmK
Caliber cm	14,91	17,26	20,3
Barrel Length cm	569	690	1215
Elevation °	10/45	10/45	10/47
Traverse °	360	360	360
Weight tonnen	74	80	86,1
Gun Length m	20,1	20,1	18,45
Max Velocity m/s	805	875	925
Max Range km	22,5	26,8	36,4
Rounds/hr	80	60	30
Shell Weight kg	43	62,7	112/122

	21cmK 12	24cmK Th.B.	28cmK kz.B.
Caliber cm	21,1	23,8	28,3
Barrel Length, cm	3330	840	1120
Elevation °	25/50	10/45	10/45
Traverse °	360	1/360	1/360
Weight tonnen	302	95	129
Gun Length m	41,4	20,7	22,8
Max Velocity m/s	1625	675	820
Max Range km	115	20,2	29,5
Rounds/hr	6	15	10
Shell Weight kg	107,5	150	240

The barrel of the 24 cm L/35 gun "Theodor Bruno" is in horizontal loading position as the ammunition hoist raises a shell for loading. The barrel cradle is a cast two-piece structure, and there are two hydraulic recoil systems.

24 cm

[Below] Drawing of a 24 cm "Theodor Bruno." Note that this version has a different gun carriage and barrel design. During the First World War, guns of this type used large stabilizers to take the weight of the gun carriage off the railroad bogie trucks, a very unusual system.

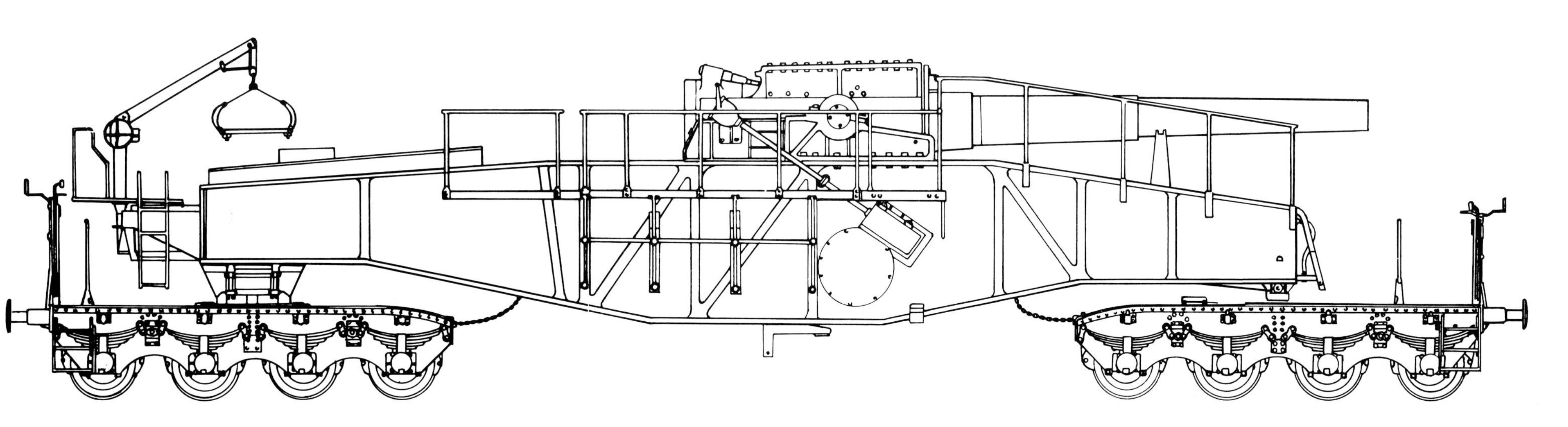

In a railroad yard in the West, probably at Lüttich, three 24 cm "Theodor Bruno" railroad guns have been camouflaged to hide their firing positions. By being covered to look like cars carrying bulky loads, the guns were difficult to detect from a distance–only the shell hoist cranes gave away their exact positions.

[Below left] Heavy camouflage was necessary for these large guns, because firing sites often were limited in some military situations, they could be seen from the air when not camouflaged, and there was a shortage of flak units available to defend the guns. Effective camouflage for this 24 cm "Theodor Bruno" meant the difference between life and death.

Here the gun has been emplaced on a turntable. At the right is the ammunition carrier, which ran on the same circular track used by the turntable. In the foreground is the narrow gauge track for the reserve ammunition cars used to resupply the gun with shells from the main supply train.

Here the extensive camouflage frame and netting are being erected over the gun. It was a time consuming job, and had to be done every time the weapon was moved and emplaced, and was also often done during periods between firing from the same position. The VÖGELE turntable was needed to provide traverse with a fixed carriage.

[Below right] The loaders have pushed the next seven 150 kg shells up to the gun on a shell car, using the turntable circular track. The shell on the right has been placed in a loading cradle.

This raised ammunition cart, built by the gun crew, carried the shells at the same level as the gun's loading platform, making loading easier. Here is a particularly good view of the use of the turntable track to carry the ammunition cars.

The loaders have placed a shell into the clamp of the loading crane, and it will then be lifted up to the loading cradle behind the breech. Note the rotating bands on the projectiles. These engaged the rifling in the barrel to rotate the shell to stabilize it, and also to form an effective gas seal for the best range.

Two loaders winch up a shell with the loading crane-almost 3 meters from the loading car to the gun breech.

[Below right] Traversing the 94 tonne carriage and turntable of the 24 cm "Theodor Bruno" required several men, even with the help of the geared traversing mechanism. The gun laying officer communicated with the gun commander for the correct azimuth bearing and signaled the crew when the weapon was aimed at the target.

Here the loading crane crew lowers the shell onto the loading cradle, which is then pushed up to the breech so that the shell can be rammed into the breech. After that, the propellant was loaded and the breech was closed.

Here the gun crew rams the propellant casing into the breech prior to firing. Note the second shell and propellant case on the loading cradle, ready to be loaded for the following shot.

The loading ramrod is passed aside prior to closing the breech. Shown is a rear view of the loading cradle with the next shell and case. The barrel was lowered to the horizontal "loading" position after each shot, as all loading operations had to be conducted with barrel horizontal.

After loading, the barrel is elevated to the correct angle for the desired range. This photo also shows some details of the VÖGELE turntable and the circular traversing track. The heavy counterweight over the rear of the barrel was a characteristic detail of the 24 cm "Theodor Bruno" railroad guns.

While the barrel is being elevated, the loaders prepare the next shell on the loading cradle. This view of the gun and turntable shows the relatively short barrel, which made this design outmoded compared to later guns.

A view of the gun just after the weapon has been fired–note the cloud of dust in front of the gun, raised by the muzzle blast. Next the barrel will be lowered to the horizontal "loading" position and the shell and propellant charge on the loading cradle will be pushed into the breech for the next shot.

Another view of the "Theodor Bruno" 24 cm gun just after firing. The crewmen have covered their ears to protect them from the pressure of the muzzle blast. In the foreground is part of the turntable traversing track.

The 28 cm railroad gun "Kürze Bruno" ["Short Bruno"] was built from 1936 to 1938, a total of 8 guns being completed. They were assigned to four batteries [690, 694, 695, 696], each having two guns, and later these were joined by the E-battery 721, which was equipped with two captured guns. The 28 cm "Kurze Bruno" weighed 45.5 tonnen, had a barrel length of 11.2 meters, a maximum elevation of 45°, and a maximum range of 29.5 km. During the First World War, this type of gun used a sunken turntable which could be locked in position. By lowering the gun carriage onto the turntable, the load on the wheels was reduced and the gun could be fully traversed.

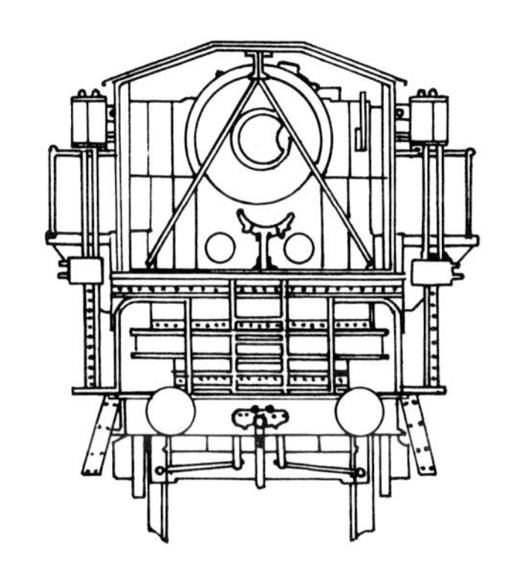

28 cm

A side view plan of the 28 cm "Kürze Bruno" L/40, showing the screwjacks used to raise and lower the carriage; these were later eliminated. Note the covered shelter for the gun crew and ready ammunition, at the left end of the carriage.

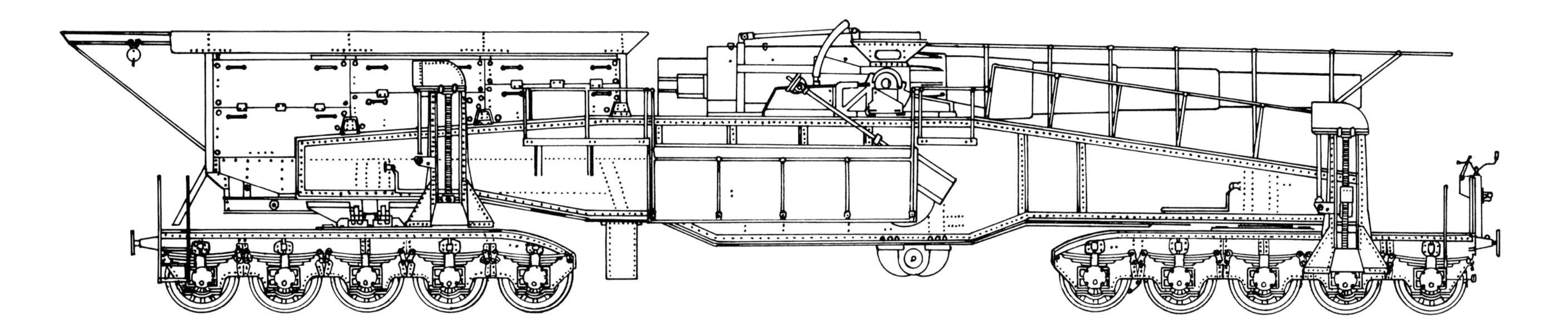

A 28 cm "Kürze Bruno" L/40 with the barrel in the loading position. The ammunition is brought up to the gun in ammunition cars, and are then transfered to a shell carrier car that ran on the circular turntable track. The muzzle velocity was 820 m/sec., and the muzzle energy was 8220 meter/tonnen. The maximum rate of fire was 10 rounds per hour.

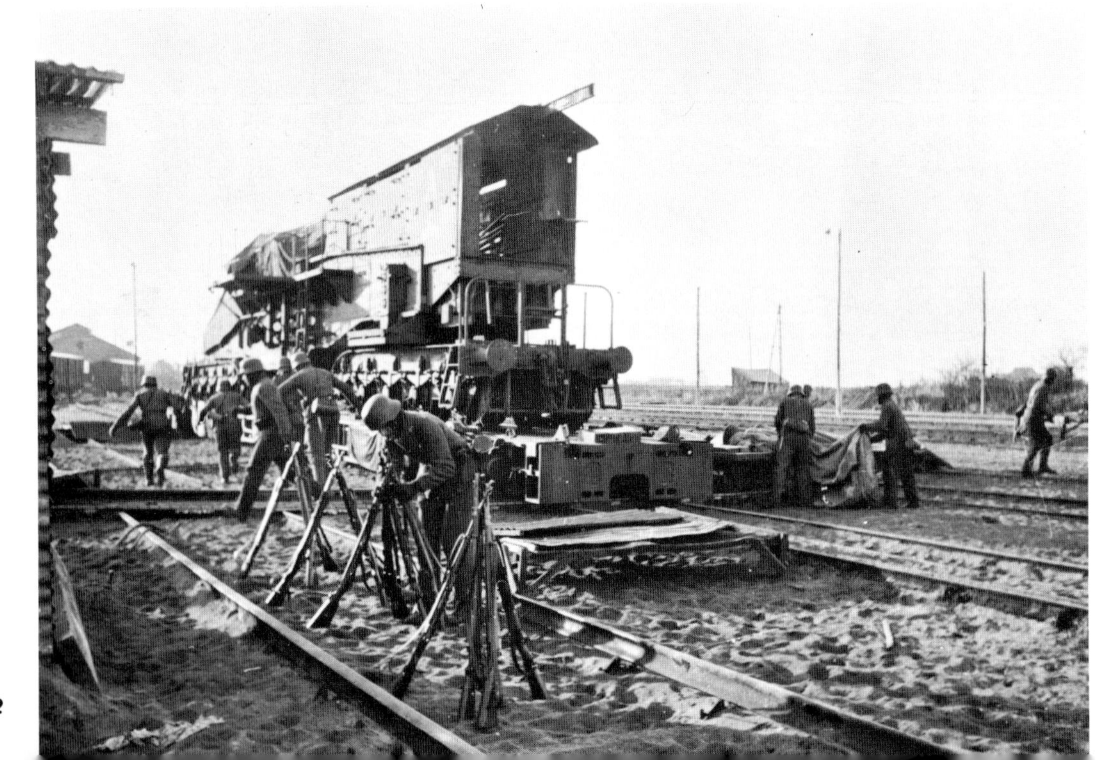

A rear view of a "Kürze Bruno", shown as the crew prepares to man the gun. The gun weighed 129.5 tonnen, and like the older "Bruno" models, was 22.8 m long. The "Kürze Bruno" was the first of four types of 28 cm railroad guns—all constructed using naval barrels from the 1920's. All had two 5-axle railroad trucks.

A front view of "Kürze Bruno" in firing position. The muzzle is nearly 15 meters above the gun carriage. Note the stepped construction of these older naval barrels.

The left gun of a "Kürze Bruno" battery on the Belgian Channel coast at the moment of firing. The gun is on a turntable and the recoil buffer on the table will control the recoil run of the gun carriage. The shield for the gun crew afforded only minimal protection from enemy fire. This site has no attempts at camouflage, and this indicates that the Germans had air superiority—thus attack from the air was unlikely.

The camouflage framework for this 28 cm "Schwere Bruno" ["Heavy Bruno"] L/42 railway gun was used to disguise the weapon during travel. The outer cover was removed, then this wood and metal frame was removed to prepare the weapon for firing. The 28 cm "Schwere Bruno" weighed 118 tonnen, had a barrel length of 11.93 meters and an overall length of 22.8 meters. Two guns were assigned to E-battery 689, with the velocity measuring troop 613 as a companion unit.

Here crewmen have removed the muzzle cap which kept the barrel clean and free of foreign objects during travel from one site to another. Note the camouflage netting and framework still erected on the breech area in the rear.

15cm-Kanone[E] of the EisbBttr "Gneisenau" manned by Kriegsmarine personnel, on the Invasion Front, 1944. Reichsbahn Grey with camouflage nets.

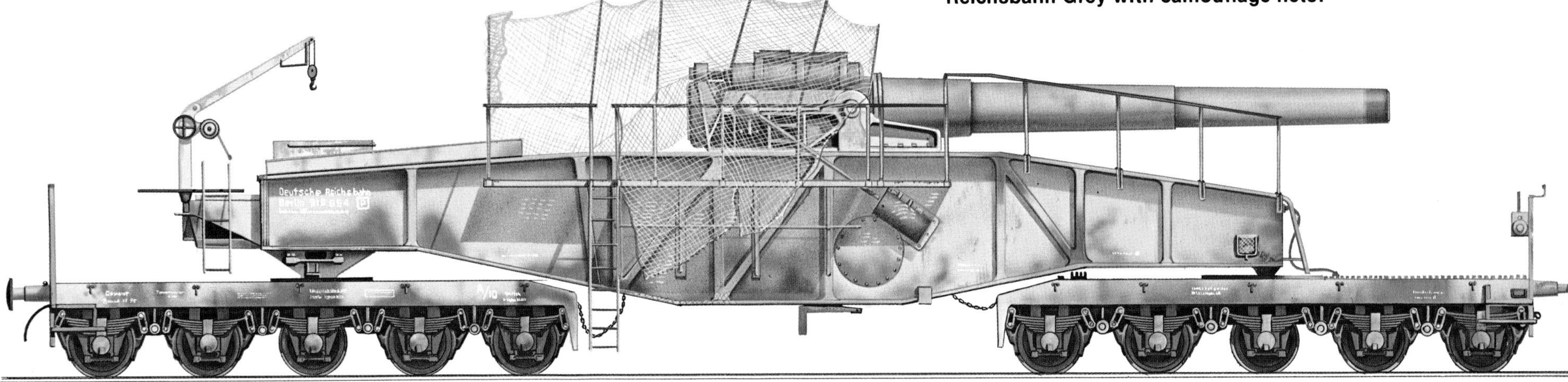

28cm-Kanone[E] "Schwere Bruno" of EisbBttr 689, Channel Coast, 1944. Sand Yellow over Reichsbahn Grey with camouflage net.

28cm-Kanone 5[E] "Leopold" or "Anzio Annie" Italy, 1944. Dark Brown over Dark Sand.

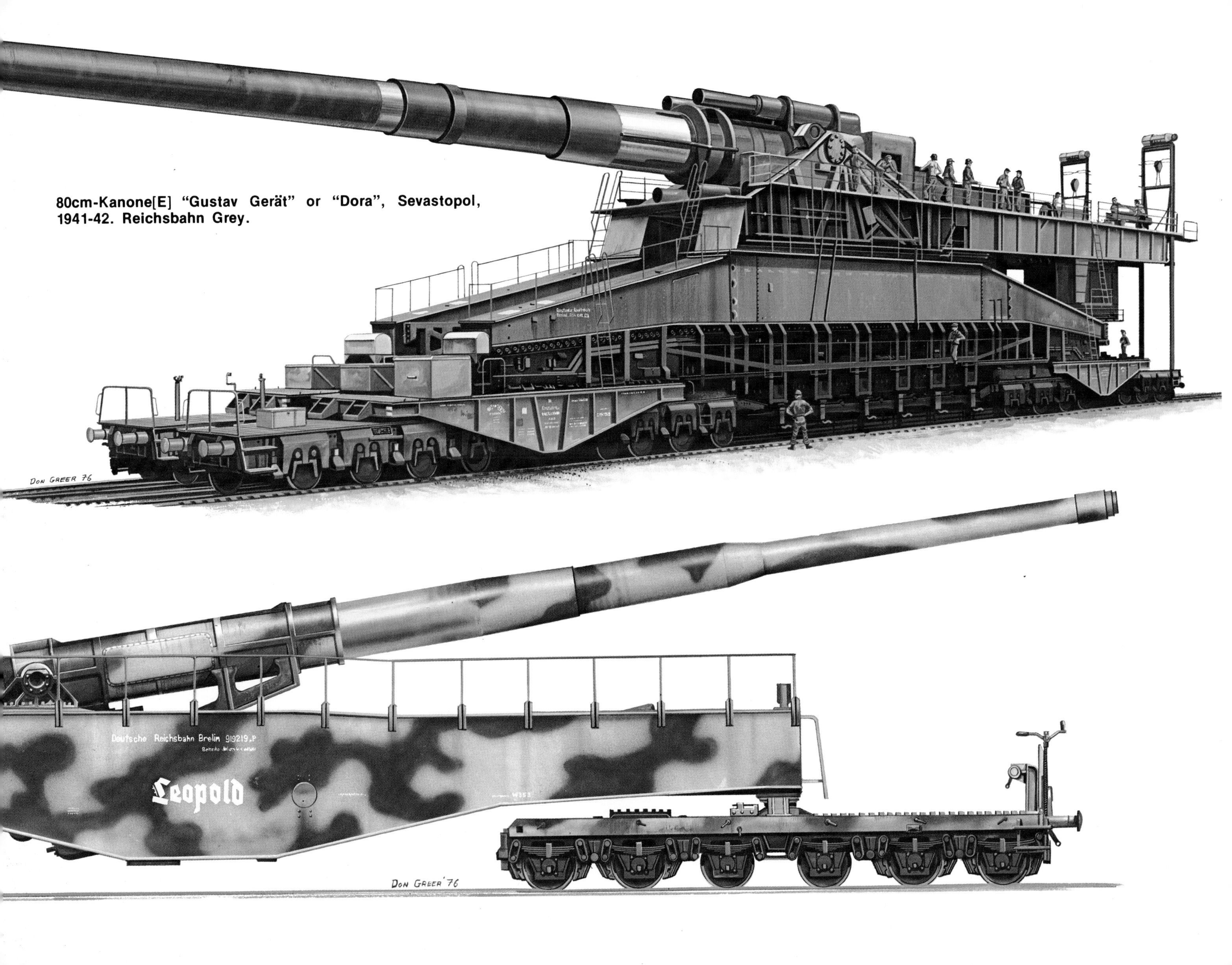

80cm-Kanone[E] "Gustav Gerät" or "Dora", Sevastopol, 1941-42. Reichsbahn Grey.

While a gun layer checks the angle of elevation of this “Schwere Bruno,” another crewman sets the safety lock on the trigger mechanism. Just barely visible on the rear face of the breech name “FRIEDRICH KRUPP” and the 3-ring symbol of Krupp. Also stamped on the breech were the barrel number and year of manufacture.

A view through the open breech, showing the firing chamber and the rifling in the barrel. The rifling rotated to the right increasing from 2° to 4°. The muzzle velocity was 820-875 m/sec.

The crew runs to man a "Schwere Bruno" during an alarm in the E-battery 689. Here is a rear view of the gun, showing how much of the camouflage frame and netting has been left on the gun. Again a VÖGELE turntable is used for full traverse. Camouflage netting has been draped over the turntable track to conceal it.

In spite of their design's dating from World War I, the Bruno series of 28 cm guns [basically enlarged and reinforced versions of the 24 cm type] served to increase the number of operational railroad guns without a lengthy development period. 13 of these guns were constructed and entered service from 1936 to 1938. This is the third version with an L/92 barrel, known as "Schwere Bruno".

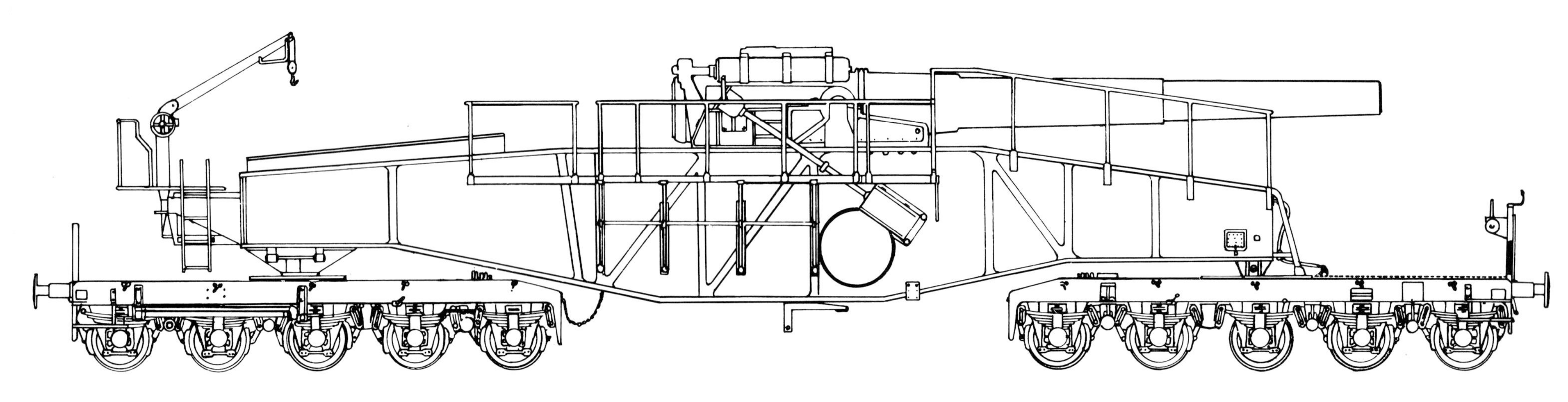

Specifications

	28cmK n.B.	28cmK 5
Caliber cm	28,3	28,3
Barrel Length cm	1640	2153,9
Elevation °	50	50
Traverse °	1	1
Weight tonnen	150	218
Gun Length m	22,8	31,1
Max Velocity m/s	955	1120
Max Range km	46,6	59
Rounds/hr	20	15
Shell Weight kg	255	255

	28cmK s.B.	80cmK Dora
Caliber cm	28,3	80
Barrel Length, cm	1193	3248
Elevation °	10/45	53
Traverse °	1/360	0
Weight tonnen	118	1350
Gun Length m	22,8	43
Max Velocity m/s	860	820
Max Range km	37,8	47
Rounds/hr	10	3
Shell Weight kg	284	4,8/7,1t

A view down the bore of a 28 cm "Schwere Bruno." The rifling grooves can be seen at the muzzle, and a shell can be seen lying in the breech.

A side view of the forward carriage and barrel of a "Schwere Bruno." This gun fired a 284 kg shell at a muzzle velocity of 860 m/sec. and reached a maximum range of 37.8 km. Interestingly enough, this performance was not matched by the 28 cm "Lange Bruno" ["Long Bruno"] in spite of its longer barrel and higher muzzle velocity with the same projectile weight.

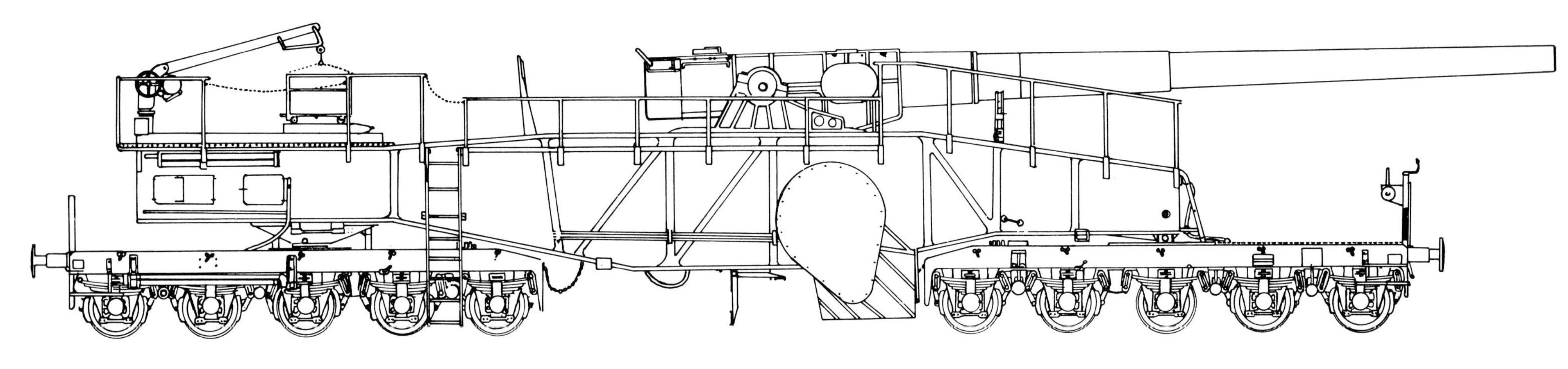

The 28 cm "Lange Bruno" was the second of the Bruno series. With an L/4: barrel, this gun showed considerable margin in performance over the "Kürz Bruno," range being increased over 6 km to 36.1 km. Three of this model wer built in 1937.

The K5[E], a 28 cm gun with an L/76 barrel, carried its total weight of 218 tonnen on two 6-axle bogie trucks. Developed during 1934-1936, tested from 1936, and introduced into troop service from 1940, the K5[E] was a completely new design which represented the best railroad gun used in WW 2 by the German artillery troops. 25 K5[E] weapons were built, and became the standard German railroad gun; almost half of the German railroad guns were 28 cm. The K5[E] was popularly known to German troops as "Schlanke Berta" ["Slim Berta"] or "hack weapon." Allied troops pinned down on the Anzio beachhead, and subjected to the shelling of the K5[E] for many weeks, called the gun "Anzio Annie" or the "Anzio Express." During the advance out of the Anzio beachhead, two 28 cm K5's were captured by American troops when railroad tracks were destroyed, preventing the Germans from withdrawing them. Both guns were destroyed, but one was later repaired and tested.

The 28 cm "Neue Bruno" ["New Bruno"] was developed from 1938 to 1940, then from 1940 to 1942, three guns were introduced into service. With a barrel 58 calibers long [L/58 = 58 x bore diameter], and a total weight of 123 tonnen, the maximum range was increased to 46.6 km. The gun carriage was a cleaner, more modern design, and both elevation and loading were hydraulically powered. The recoil cylinders were housed beneath the rectangular outer barrel casing.

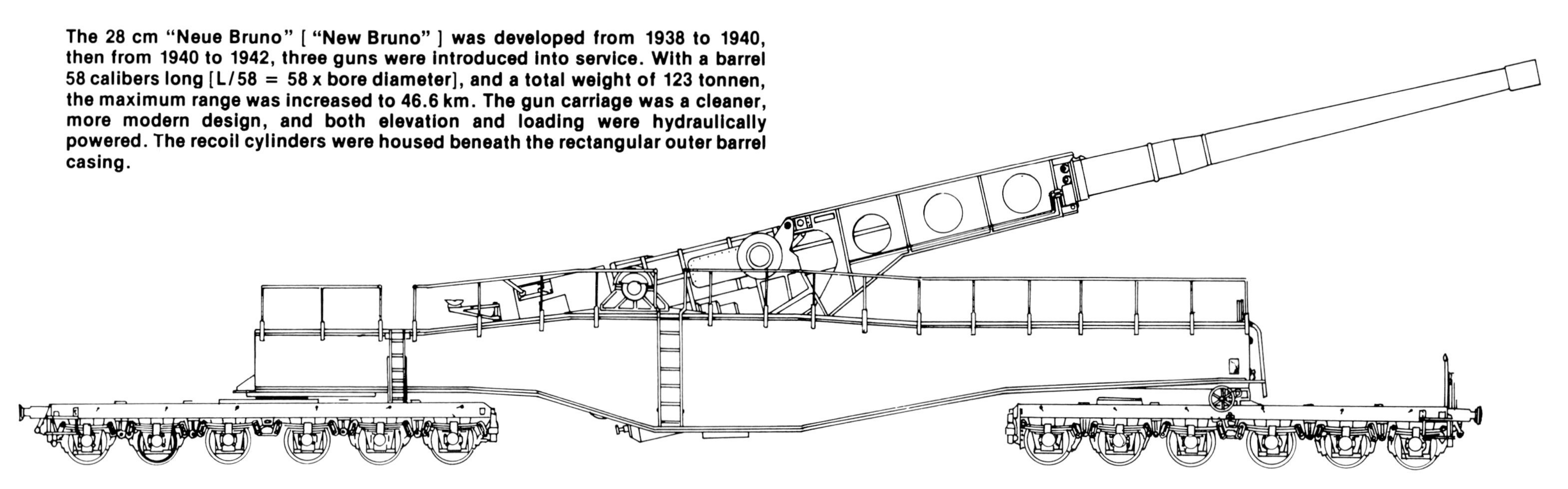

The barrel of the 28 cm K5[E] had a length of 21.54 meters, and was manufactured in four versions; the differences were in the rifling design: 10 mm deep rifling; 7 mm deep rifling; multigroove rifling with a conical bore; and smooth bore of 31 cm diameter. The barrel was mounted in a special cradle, and maximum range was 59-62 km. with a muzzle velocity of 1120 m/sec. 8-15 shells could be fired per hour; each shell weighed 255 kg. The barrel liner lasted from 240-550 rounds. In May 1943, the total order for the K5[E] was limited to 30 complete guns, 3 complete barrels, and 30 barrel liners.

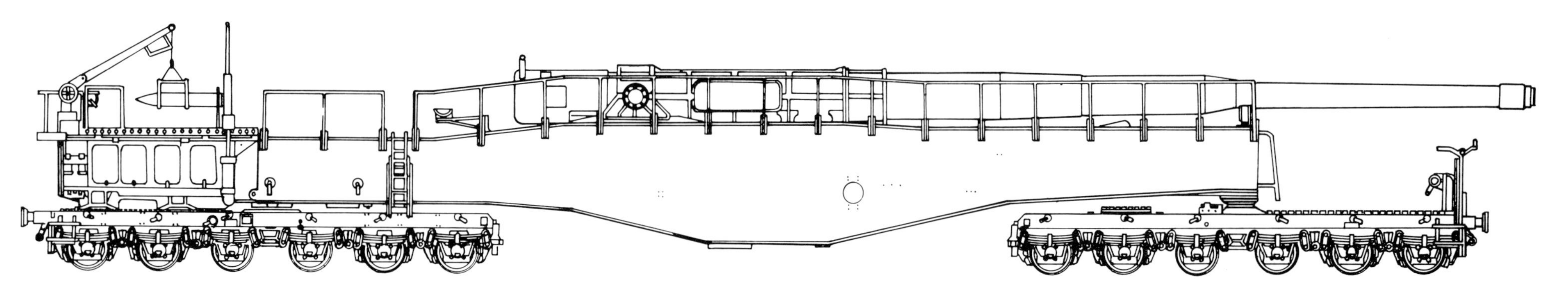

The K5(E) battery with one or two guns was transported by a complete and well-thought out system comprising two separate trains. The "gun train" had a locomotive; the K5(E) railroad gun; a ventilated ammunition car; a diesel switching locomotive used for moving ammunition cars into position, moving the cranes and the gun—when it was used on the VÖGELE turntable (the diesel was an Orenstein-Koppel model C14, weighing 40 tonnen and capable of 60 km.hr.); two shell cars (each carried 113 rounds, each weighing 255 kg); two propellant charge cars; one equipment car with small tools and supplies; one armored railroad car for defense of the gun crew using small arms; one kitchen and supply car; one fire control car (blast proof); one flat car with a 2 cm Flakvierling 38 for air defense and 3 buses for the reconnaissance and quarter-master units. That was followed by the "turntable train" with a locomotive; one car for each section of the 29.46 meter diameter turntable, which was divided in the center drive section; another car carrying the 16 sections for the circular traverse track for the turntable and the construction crane; a car with rail and track fittings; three more ammunition cars; a supply and tool car; a flak car; and 9 flat cars for buses and other vehicles used by the battery.

Outside Leningrad, on 9 Oct. 1943, a 28 cm K5 [E] shows the maximum elevation of the L/76 barrel as the crew prepares to fire. The crew men behind the gun are standing on the special inclined track used when the gun was pushed up onto the turntable. Among the units in this sector were E-battery 712 [with velocity measuring troop [mot.] 697] and E-battery 713 [with velocity measuring troops 617 and 765]. From late 1943, because of enemy air superiority and the increasing destruction of the German military railway network, it was proposed to build the K5 as a field weapon by making the barrel, gun carriage, and ground support base as separate sections. Each section was to transported by two tractors [in this case, the tractors were to be Tiger II's, and each transported component weighed 130 tonnen.] In this way, the K5 was to be made independent of the railroad system and could be employed in any area where the tractors could carry it. The plan was never completed, but it marked the beginning of the end of the railroad gun.

The gunner used a long trigger lanyard to fire the K5[E]. In spite of a firing height of 3.55 meters, the total length of the gun was only 21.234 m. The barrel elevation in this photograph is 50°.

[Right] "Fire!" This shot gives an impression of the tremendous muzzle blast of the K5[E]. Note the crewmen on the ground holding their ears. To increase the maximum range, a new type of shell [RGr 4331] was developed. The RGr 4331 was a rocket-assisted projectile weighing 248 kg., and the rocket motor was ignited 19 seconds after firing, pushing the shell farther into the stratosphere and resulting in a maximum range of 86.5 km. Although it was successful, the rocket motor did limit the amount of explosive carried in the projectiles, and in addition, the test facility at Peenemünde developed a cast long arrow-shaped projectile with wings, weighing 120 kg and constructed for use with the 31 cm smoothbore barrel. The shell's stabilizing ring [sabot] held it in the barrel and formed the gas seal, but was discarded when the projectile left the barrel. Because of the greatly reduced resistance of this type of barrel, the muzzle velocity could be increased to 1524 m/sec., resulting in ranges of 155-160 km approximately 40 km more than that of the K12 [the longest range gun available]. At the end of the war, two of these guns were used against the U.S. First Army.

A 28 cm K5[E] with the highest barrel elevation [50°], seen at the Kieferwald/Pommern, East Sea coast, Rügenwalde. This gun was used by the training and replacement detachment [mot.] 100, a training and troop trials unit for railroad artillery. This gun has been placed on a VÖGELE turntable, and the circular traversing track can be seen under the ends of the table.

A K5[E] firing from a turntable on the Western front in 1945. This rear view demonstrates the relatively small target area exposed when the gun was seen end-on. Only from the side was the shape and size completely apparent.

80 cm

One of the three special transport trains for the 80 cm[E] "Dora", seen at the Leipzig railroad station before leaving for Russia, 1942. While northeast of Sevastopol, the necessary firing position was connected by a rail line to the next track, which was then expanded to a double track with a turnout [switch]. The "Dora" was so large that it required two tracks for the necessary stability and weight distribution.

The largest, and nearly the last, of the WW 2 railroad guns was the 80 cm(E) "Dora" (later called "Schwerer Gustav"--"Heavy Gustav"-from 22 June 1942). With a barrel length of 40.6 calibers (L/40.6), the "Dora"--largest and heaviest gun ever built--was as great a shock to the world as the "Paris" gun of 1918. It dwarfed every other gun used during the Second World War.

In 1935, the Oberkommando Heer (OKH) conducted tests to determine which calibers of artillery would be effective against the Maginot Line fortifications, which were of great concern to German military planners. Krupp's design department tested the possible designs of 70, 80, and 100 cm diameter. When Hitler visited the Krupp works in 1936, he demanded the development of this super heavy gun. Without waiting for further tests, the specification was established as follows; maximum range: 35-45 km.; maximum elevation: 65°; penetration capabilities: 1 meter of armor steel, 7 meters of concrete, and 30 meters of solid earth. In 1937, the design for the 80 cm gun proved to be satisfactory and the same year, the final order to begin construction was given to Professor (Dipl. Ing.) Erich Müller. In spite of much previous experience in design and production of the K12 and K5, the "Dora" was a difficult design to construct and many problems were caused by the tremendous size and weight of the gun.

The total weight of "Dora" was 1350 tonnen; overall length was 42.97 meters; the width was 7 meters; height was 11.6 meters; the barrel was 32.48 meters long and weighed 400 tonnen, and of the 400 tonnen barrel, 110 tonnen were just the breech block and breech ring. The original delivery date (spring 1940) could not be met, and as a result the invasion of France proceeded without the gun, the Maginot Line eventually being outflanked and captured intact. The attack on Gibraltar never took place, so another promising target was eliminated. The barrel was finished in 1941, and tested at the Hillersleben training ground from 10 Sept. - 6 Oct. 1941, and at Rügenwalde from 25 Nov. - 5 Dec. 1941. In 1942, the completed gun was ready for action at Rügenwalde, and was then transfered to Army Group South for action in the siege of Sevastopol. The order for action at Sevastopol was given personally to the gun's unit commander by Col.-Gen. Halder, Chief of the German General Staff. The 80 cm(E) saw its only combat action at Sevastopol, firing 48 shells at 7 targets in 5 days of firing.

[Right] The gun-transport train for the 80 cm[E] "Dora" arrived 7 days before the start of the attack in Bachtschisarei at Sevastopol. The secondary cranes and large construction crane, already in place, are in the background here. Construction started immediately with two 1000 PS diesel locomotives on adjacent parallel tracks, with especially close spacing of the ties to support the great weight during construction: note also the extra single-rail tracks built for the traveling cranes. Next came the right and left halves of the lower carriage, as 20-axle special railroad cars were moved into position, and tightly connected to form a double-track drive unit and firing platform. There were a total of 8 bogey trucks under the cars, and the gun ran on 80 wheels, almost like moving on a tank track. Each axle had to support 33.75 tonnen. At the actual firing position, the double track extended into a shooting curve for traversing the gun.

Three or four trains transported the construction crews for the gun and carriage (about 1,000 men) and one train carried the railroad pioneers, who completed the firing position and special tracks in 3-6 weeks, using approximately 1500 local workmen as laborers.

The construction of the complete gun required several loads of components, carried in several trains. The lower carriage was transported in two loads, while 5 loads were needed to accommodate the upper carriage and barrel components: breechblock, barrel cradle, trunnion pins and assemblies, barrel, and 2-piece barrel liner. The 7 loads weighed up to 700 tonnen. Included in the construction trains were cranes and 250 men of the gun battery-fitters, electricians, and track layers. In spite of the immense size of the "Dora," the prefabricated components enabled the gun and carriage to be completed in 3 days.

Here is shown one of the trunnion cradles of the upper carriage of the 80 cm "Dora"; the cradles support the barrel trunnions and transmit the recoil forces to the carriage. The maximum elevation of the barrel was 53°.

The heavy artillery unit, consisting of the one 80 cm "Dora," was commanded by Colonel (Oberst) Dipl. Engineer R. Bŏhm. It included the headquarters; headquarters battery, with a fire control section; a reinforced intelligence platoon; a surveying platoon with 4 observation units with infrared equipment and a plotting unit; and the gun battery troops for erection, service, and removal of the gun, a total of 500 men. The assigned support troops, such as construction troops; flak detachment; 20 engineers from Krupp; reinforced nebelwerfer detachment, two Rumanian guard companies; Military Police unit; dog patrol troop; plus a helicopter section and fighter cover from the Luftwaffe, came to about 3870 men. Firing the "Dora" required 350 men, because muzzle velocity and breech pressure were measured, and the propellant for the following shot was carefully chosen in order to keep the projectiles on target within a 1% dispersion error.

After the trunnion pins were fitted to the barrel cradle, the assembly was lowered onto the upper carriage. The traveling crane with the barrel cradle has been rolled nearly touching the first crane. There were four recoil cylinders to absorb the tremendous recoil forces generated by this huge weapon.

The barrel cradle for the "Dora" is shown here as it is prepared for moving from the railroad transport train to the 80 cm gun assembly point, seen in the background. Both of these huge construction cranes could be moved along the special tracks laid alongside of the main double track intended for the gun. The cranes were nearly 13 meters high, giving a good impression of the great size of the 80 cm "Dora."

The immense outer barrel, 32.48 meters long and weighing 400 tonnen, is lowered into the barrel cradle during assembly of the "Dora," using one of the hauling cranes to transport the piece and position it correctly. Next, the two-section barrel liner will be screwed together and pushed into the barrel from the rear. The breech assembly will follow that, and then the construction will be completed by the installation of the crew platforms, shell hoist, catwalks and ladders.

The 80 cm cannon [E] "Dora" moves into its prepared firing position, which has been enclosed by barbed wire fences, secured and camouflaged for several kilometers in each direction, to help conceal this huge weapon from enemy observation, and protect it from air attacks and Russian naval vessels.

The completed giant gun seen during loading operations. Here the crew is using the powered ramming gear to load one of the 80 cm projectiles into the breech. The ammunition hoists and the barrel elevation gear were operated electrically. The rammer and breechblock were operated hydraulically. Traversing the weapon was done with the two 1000 hp. diesel locomotives built into the lower carriage; they moved the gun along the firing curve. Thus, every 19-45 minutes, a shot could be fired, to a maximum range of 28-47 km. The barrel had a service life of 100 rounds fired. Two types of shells were used in the "Dora": an armor-tipped penetrating shell to pierce heavy fortifications and other substantial targets, and a high explosive shell for general bombardment use. The armor-tipped shell weighed 7.1 tonnen; the high-explosive projectile weighed 4.8 tonnen. There were three propellant charges, weighing between 1.85 to 2 tonnen. Including the propellant charge casings, the armored projectiles had a length of 6.79 meters, and the high explosive shells, a length of 8.26 meters. At the moment of firing, the recoil force increased the axle loading to 64 tonnen, resulting in the track settling 3-5 cm.

A rear view of the "Dora" 80 cm railroad gun, showing the two shell hoists, the three-story built-up construction, and the upper platforms for the gun crew—a significant achievement in the design and prefabricated construction of such a large weapon. In spite of its technical success, the "Dora" enjoyed only minor tactical success. Its design mission—the reduction of the Belgian forts and the Maginot Line—never came about due to the delays in completing the weapon. After the limited action at Sevastopol in 1942, the "Dora" appeared outside Warsaw in 1944, and then vanished in the turbulent final months of the war.

The outer barrel of the 80 cm gun, disassembled for transport, and seen in 1945 at the end of the war. The American soldier inspecting the left section provides an idea of the size of the barrel.

In 1945, a British sergeant admires a 7.1 tonne armor-capped projectile and the 1.3 meter high main propellant casing of the 80 cm "Dora" railroad gun. Today, this projectile is on display outside the Ordnance Museum building at Aberdeen Proving Ground. At first glance it appears to be a very large aerial bomb.

The muzzle end of the barrel liner for the 80 cm "Dora", seen in 1945. In mid-April, 1945, one of these 80 cm guns was blown up in Metzenhof by Grafenwöhr, before the entry of American troops. None of the guns survived the war intact.

CAPTURED GUNS

With captured and surrendered guns—most of these were of French origin—the operational stocks of German railroad guns were expanded after 1940.

Two 30.5 cm railroad guns[f] M93/06 Batignolles in a railroad station in the West, 1940. The gun in front shows the outdated design of the carriage, which was a box platform built up over the railroad trucks. Note the flatcar—at the far left—that was coupled to the end of the gun carriage to provide clearance for the long barrel.

A 32 cm railroad gun[f] M74 [in front] and a 32 cm Schneider gun [behind], seen in a railroad yard. France had developed a great variety of railroad guns during and after WW I, and the Germans took over an impressive collection of these weapons, many of which were of modern, efficient design. The gun calibers ranged from 27.4 cm to 52 cm, and since most of these were not used in German-designed weapons, the supplies of French ammunition proved as valuable as the guns themselves.

Three French railroad gun transport trains in a marshalling yard. At the left is a 34 cm M12[f] gun; in the center, a 32 cm M74[f]; and to the right, a 32 cm Schneider[f] railroad gun. After the capitulation by France, about 20 French railway guns were taken into German service, gradually becoming more and more active from 1942 onward. Most of these guns were used in France.

A right front view of a 32 cm M93[f] on the carriage of a 32 cm M74 [sliding lower structure]. Behind this gun is the carriage of a second weapon, which has had the barrel removed—note the open trunnion mounts.

The same railroad gun as on p. 43, seen from the left front side, showing the integrated design of the main gun carriage with its removable trunnion mounts, a noteworthy feature which greatly simplified maintenance.

A rear view of a 32 cm M93[f] rail gun, showing the massive breech with the manufacturer's marks and serial number. This gun had an obsolete, hand-operated locking system, using interrupted screw threads for locking. This was a common method of locking naval guns and is used to this day on naval weapons. The breech on this M93[f] was swung closed with the handle at top, then the side crank was turned, operating the worm gear which rotated the breech plug to engage the interrupted screw threads and lock the breech.

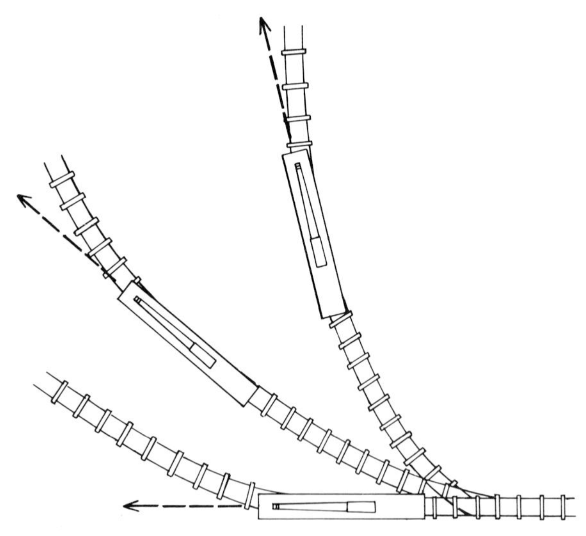

Diagram showing the use of curved track to aim the gun in several directions. Either curved track or curved sidings on a straight track could be used. The curve tangent from the axis of the gun and carriage could range from 2° up to 15°—more of a tangent curve risked lateral instability during recoil.

A right rear view of a 32 cm M74[f] with a heavily reinforced built-up barrel. This gun and carriage weighed 162 tonnen and measured 25.9 meters in length.

The 32 cm M74[f] from the rear left side, showing the relatively modern carriage design and the two 5-axle end bogie trucks. The maximum elevation was 40°, but there was no carriage traversing—this required a turntable or curved track.

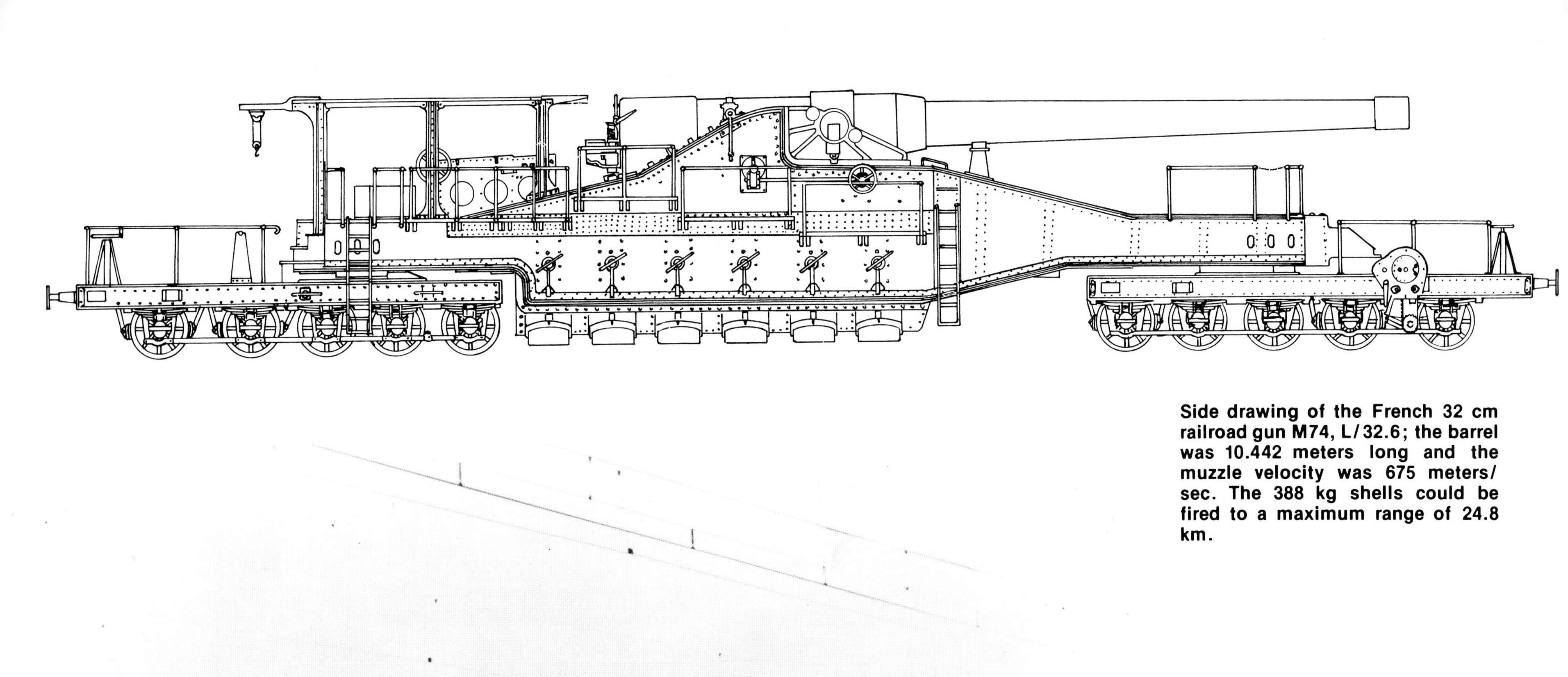

Side drawing of the French 32 cm railroad gun M74, L/32.6; the barrel was 10.442 meters long and the muzzle velocity was 675 meters/sec. The 388 kg shells could be fired to a maximum range of 24.8 km.

A 34cm railway gun[f] M12, L/47, a relatively modern gun carriage design, seen in service with railroad gun battery 674. The gun weighed 270 tonnen, was 33.73 meters long, and had a barrel length of 16.14 meters. Maximum angle of elevation was 37°, and with a muzzle velocity of 927 meters/sec., the 430 kg shells could be fired to a maximum distance of 37.6 km, which compared favorably with many of the contemporary German designs.

This 37 cm French railroad gun, seen in German service, has just been fired—note the traces of smoke still coming from the muzzle. The barrel has been lowered to the horizontal loading position, and a well-trained crew could reload a weapon like this in a few minutes, allowing several rounds to be fired within an hour.

These shells for the 37 cm French railroad gun—seen on the previous page—were about 1.60 meters long, and have been laid out along this planked deck so that they can be rolled up to the gun as quickly as the crew can fire and reload.

[Above] This gun—the same type—is the 37 cm [f] M15, and has an old type of box-shaped gun carriage, not as developed as later designs. Two of these weapons served with railroad gun battery 711, and proved to be effective weapons despite their age.

[Right] A 37 cm gun[f] on 13 Jan. 1945 in the Weichsel fires on advancing Russian troops, at maximum elevation. Again the smoke from the muzzle shows that this gun has just fired a shell.

Railroad guns never were capable of being used in a strictly tactical sense since they were too large, and their design was intended for strategic use. They had only a small role in deciding the outcome of any campaigns or battles even though they were capable of great destruction. Nonetheless, these guns—especially the later advanced types such as the K12 and K5—were very well thought out designs able to deliver heavy shells accurately over very great distances, which was the primary mission of long range artillery.

For this, these guns required the best designers and the latest advances in artillery design and technology. Like all large and advanced devices, they inspired a certain awe because of their size, and also because of the great destructive power they could deliver. The use of railroad equipment to move and service these huge weapons only added to the attraction they had due to their size. German designers and ballistics experts, along with the production workers at Krupp, accomplished great advances in artillery development within a very short time, and produced some of the finest long-range guns ever made. Unfortunately, the Germans could not agree on building large numbers of standard guns, with the result that many different types of guns were constructed, and many of these were extremely complex and costly, culminating in the truly incredible 80 cm "Dora"/"Schw. Gustav," which cost 10 million Reichsmarks each. Thus, the successes in action were limited for many of these weapons. The best of them, however, will be remembered for many years as a high point in the history of artillery design.

The era of the railroad gun was ended by the development and service use of motorized heavy field artillery, expanded air power with larger planes and bombs, and by the introduction of large long-range rockets. The ballistic missile in particular held the promise of being able to carry very large payloads over great distances, while needing relatively simple equipment for launching.

Improved methods of reconnaissance, especially by aircraft, made it nearly impossible to hide a soldier, much less a 200 tonne artillery piece 4-5 meters high, and of necessity confined to a highly visible railroad track. It is doubtful that any railroad guns still exist in the Soviet Union, especially since the Russians have in every decade since the end of WW II built new and more effective, larger rockets and missiles. The only surviving German railroad gun is the 28 cm K5(E) "Leopold" at Aberdeen Proving Ground--the lone survivor of an interesting but obsolete period in the field of artillery design and construction.

A view of a 28 cm "Kürze Bruno," L/40, seen as the shell leaves the barrel. The muzzle blast and smoke would have been disadvantages at shorter ranges. The recoil travel was only 69-75 cm, and the barrel lasted for about 850 shots before needing replacement.

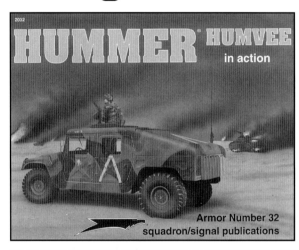

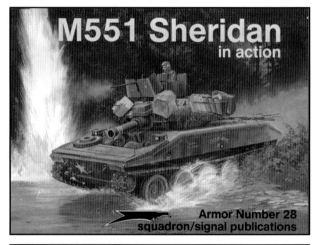

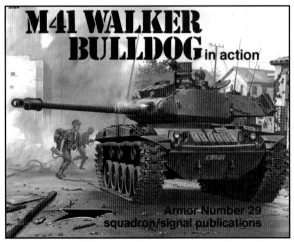

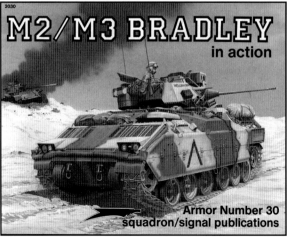

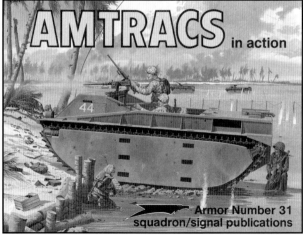